Skeletons in the Closet
Kid's Book on Archaeology
Tools You Use!
Children's Archaeology Books

pfiffikus

EDUCATIONAL BOOKS FOR CHILDREN K-12

Archaeology is the science of studying history by examining the remains of people and other things from the past.

These remains include coins, tools, structures, bones and other ancient objects. They are called artifacts.

People
who study
archaeology
are called
archaeologists.

Archaeologists dig up the ground carefully and in an organized manner to record everything they find and where those items were found.

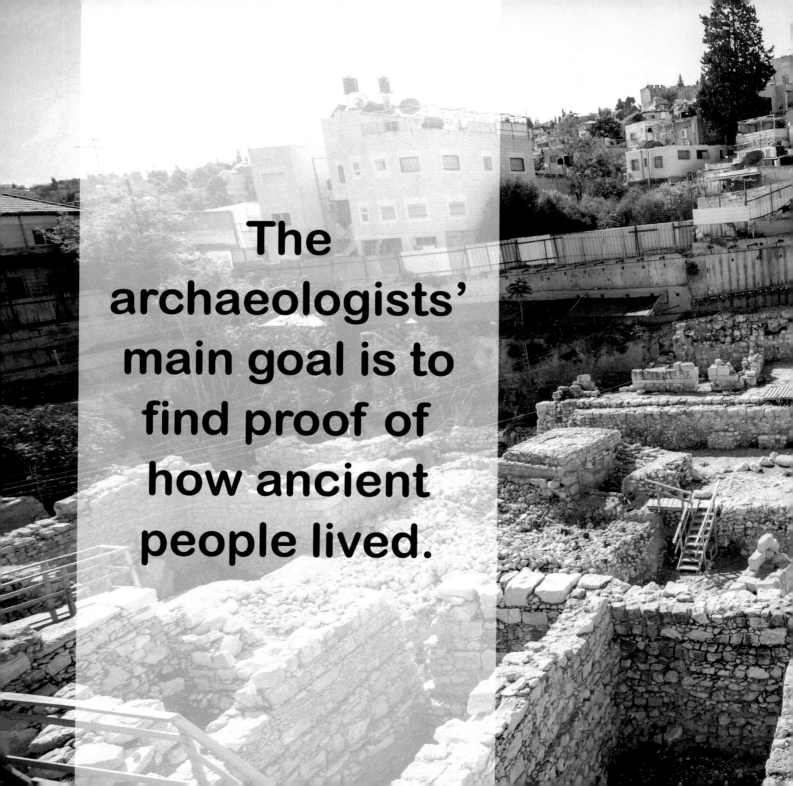

The archaeologists' main goal is to find proof of how ancient people lived.

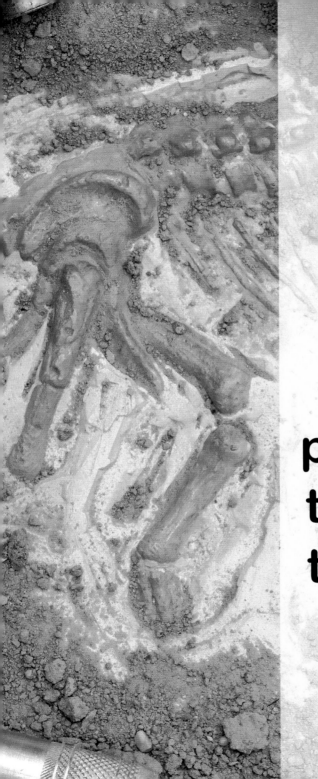

Archaeologists use many tools to dig up a potential historical site. In the next few pages, we will go through some of the tools used in the excavation process.

The pick and the shovel are tools used for digging and splitting rocks open.

The whisk and the dustpan are used to brush away dirt from artifacts.

The knife is a tool used to cut away rope or vines so archaeologists can easily see what they want to see.

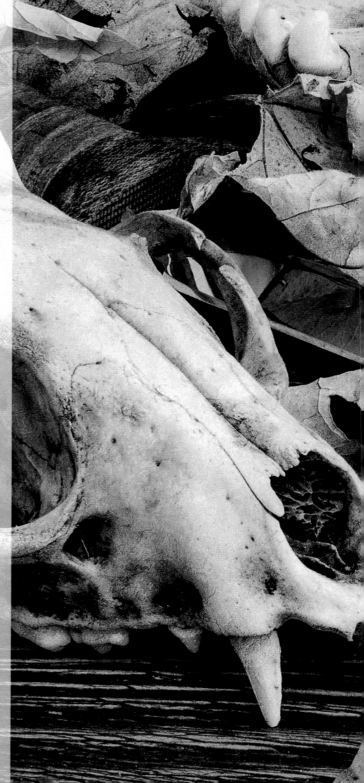

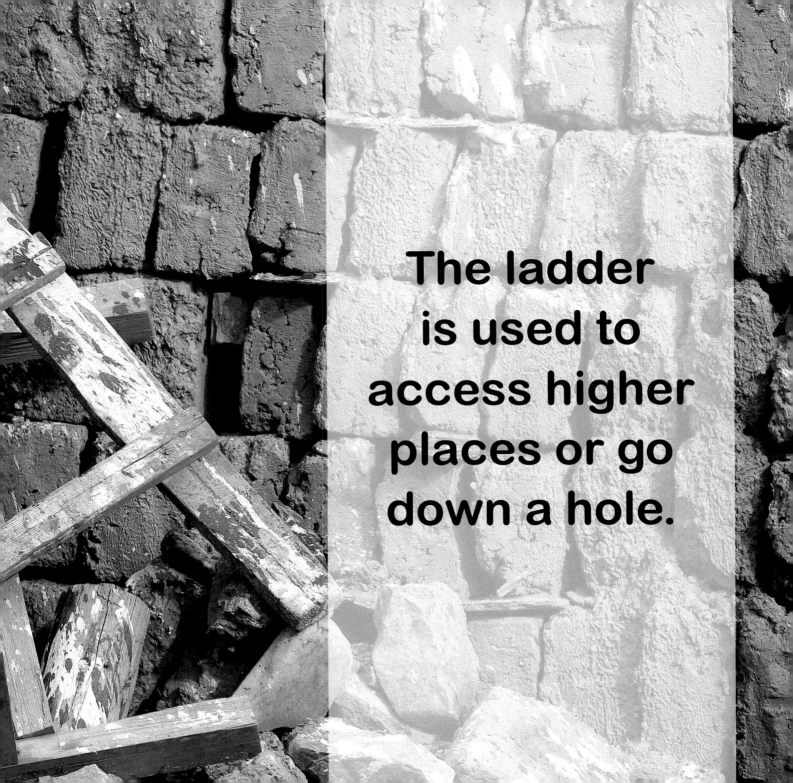

The ladder is used to access higher places or go down a hole.

The wheelbarrow is used to transport big and heavy artifacts from one place to another.

The pencil and notebook are must-haves for archaeologists. These are used to record any information about the artifacts found.

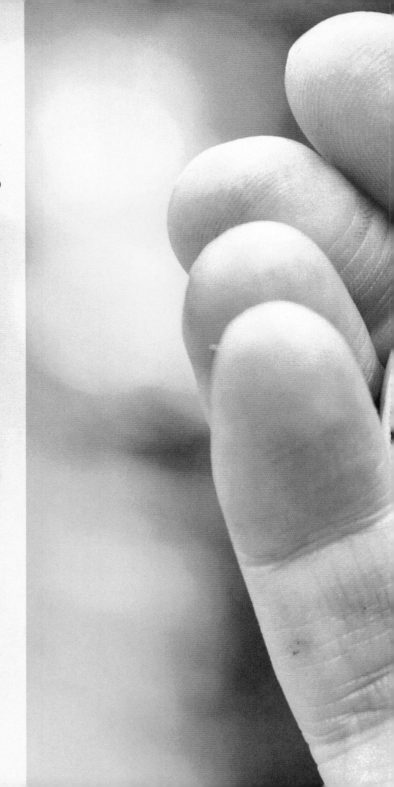

The compass
is important
to know
the exact
location
of where
artifacts
were found.

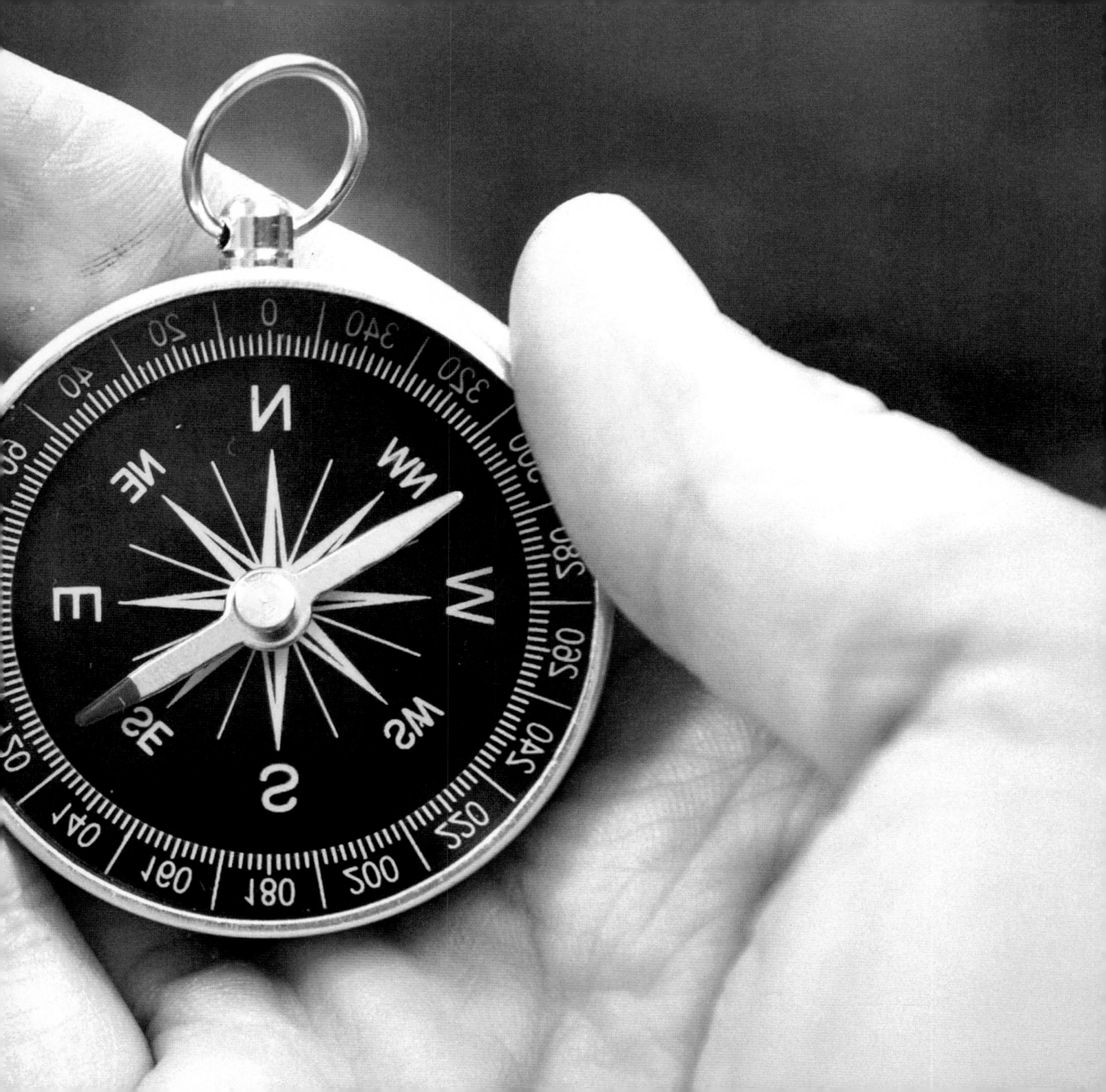

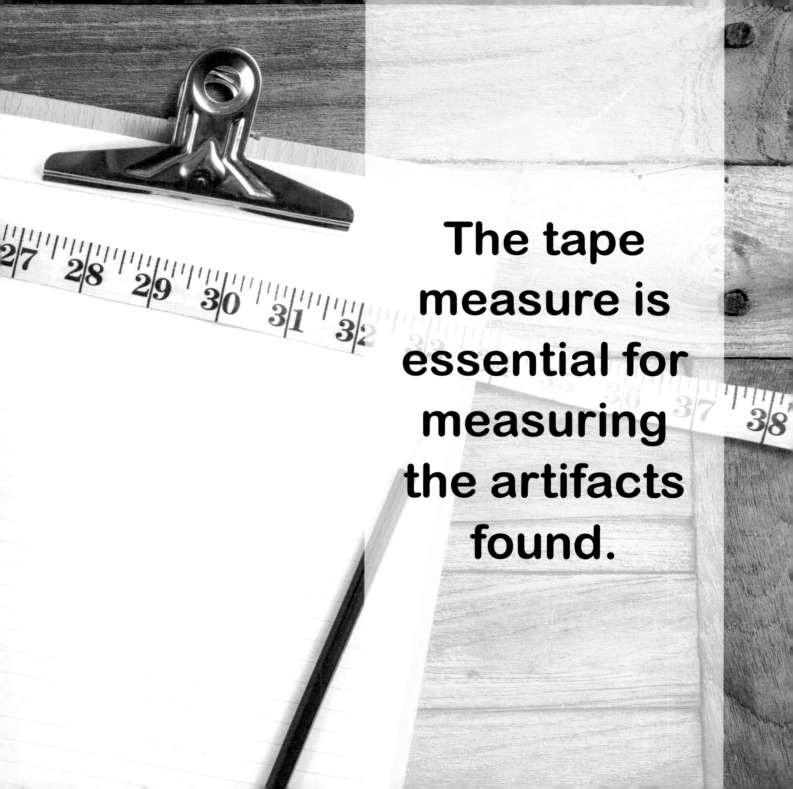

The tape measure is essential for measuring the artifacts found.

Some special telescopes as well are used by archaeologists to see things that are far away.

Gloves should be used by archaeologists to keep their hands safe and to protect the artifacts from being damaged during handling.

Helmets keep archaeologists' heads safe.

The first aid kid is important for emergency purposes.

There are more tools that can be used by an archaeologist. Research and have fun!

Made in the USA
San Bernardino, CA
01 December 2019